How to Survive a

MASS SHOOTING!

10 steps that may save your life from an active shooter

Walter Hebrew

DISCLAIMER

Actual experiences inspired this work! You may receive help from this work or you may not. Due to the nature of an individual's effort, no universal claims of help accompany this work. Your use or inability to use the information inside of this work predicates on your personal efforts. The author/publisher nor any of its affiliates (sellers, distributors, marketers, etc...) will not be liable for any special, indirect, incidental, consequential or punitive damages. Nor any other damages whatsoever arising out of your use or inability to use this work or any information, products or services of the author/publisher, whether based on contractual, statutory, tort or other grounds. In any case or situation, the author/publisher will only be responsible for the price paid for this work per the refund policy and terms. Your use of this work acknowledges your understanding and acceptance to this disclaimer.

Other Works by Walter Hebrew

Negroes in my Attic

How to Survive a Mass Shooting!: 10 steps that may save your life from an active shooter

Original content by Walter Hebrew. Book content, cover, layout and design copyright protected. All rights reserved.

Published by

HOOD THEOREM™

INTRO

This little work is about how to survive a mass shooting. Taking steps listed in this book may help save a life. There are no guarantees that accompanies this information but providing this information will help a person think about how to survive if ever in a situation where mass shooting occurs.

Avoidance of mass crowds, events, and situations is primary if you want to prevent being in a mass shooting situation, however if you must be among the masses there are particular things you can do in order to enhance your chances of survival. The perspective herein is one that derives from a mid to large size inner city upbringing in the United States where crowd shootings happened often at sporting events, clubs, and parties. Yes, I said often. Eventually, I was able to improve my life and my surroundings and was not subject to such foolish environments.

Sometimes the shooting incidents were documented, but many times not.

Unbelievably, mass shootings were commonplace in the environment I grew up, so I was able to develop certain aspects that helped me survive that time of my life. What I learned will help many since we are living in an era where mass shootings can happen anywhere and not just the inner city. I would like to share my knowledge in this little work with the hopes that it may save a life.

GAME NIGHT

"Get down Walter, get the FUCK down!" My best friend yelled at me before pushing me to the ground. Gunshots heard in multiples surrounded the outside of a high school football game. The game was over and hundreds of people stood around post-game socializing about the lopsided score before the sounds of fear persisted for a few minutes.

On the ground, my heart raced extremely fast as others ran passing me by. It was pandemonium. There was no warning, no confrontations, and no justifications; it was not a rivalry game or other crazy reason, just gunshots from a car passing by.

It was the first time I experienced such a scary incident. Yes, I said scary. It was crazy scary. I was only 15 years old at the time. I can remember begging my folks to let me go to the game. It would be the first time that I had ever gone to an event with my friend by ourselves. For something like a shooting to take place the first time with that responsibility, really had an influence on my life. I discussed for days what happened that Saturday with anyone that would listen. Before I knew it, a week had passed and it was time for another game.

My friend asked if I was going and immediately my survival instincts took over. I was a teenager enamored with the joy of going to school activities and having fun so worrying about shootings was a very tough thought process on my young mind. What if there is another shooting at the game? Will I be lucky to miss bullets again? How many people are going to the game? Will the school provide more security? How will I escape if somebody starts to shoot? Can I know beforehand if a shooting is going to happen? Is it worth attending?

These questions and many others persisted in the mind of a teenager. Innately, survival instincts kicked in. Refusing or not going to events, parties, and activities as a teenager seemed unrealistic at the time. Not knowingly, natural steps on how to survive a mass shooting developed in my mind and over time, well into adulthood, those steps matriculated into techniques and

How to Survive a Mass Shooting

ideologies that may help anyone anywhere survive a mass shooting.

Some steps are more significant than others are. You may know a few; you may not. I tapered it down to only ten steps I did and still do in order to survive a mass shooting. These steps may look to appear in chronological order but they are not in any order of importance. All steps listed herein have served an important purpose with the survival of a mass shooting.

How to Survive a Mass Shooting

STEP

#1

How to Survive a Mass Shooting

GET AN UNDERSTANDING

You have to understand the type of event you attend. Mass shootings occur at many different events and functions, but understanding the event such as how many people will be there, the location of the event, the types of people at the event, the level of security, the time of day of the event, and how long the event will last, will help your survival mindset before you go.

Whatever you do or wherever you go with a great number of people, you must get full understanding of the event. Whenever I went to games after the first shooting, I always found out what teams were playing, if leaving the game slightly early was an option, what seating section is available, escape route, etc...

Mindful questions such as those are your first line of defense. As with someone that may experience culture shock, understanding your environment (Dealing with Cultural Shock, 2016) is important to survive a mass shooting. Your enjoyment and good time will not be in peril by you getting a good understanding of the event so do this BEFOREHAND.

Step

#2

How to Survive a Mass Shooting

BE ON HIGH ALERT

Self-high alertness is necessary to survive any shooting event. High-alert mode is one-step away from having paranoia. Simply put, you must act as your own security by being self-aware of ALL surroundings, people, and circumstances. You should not depend solely on event security and others for your personal safety.

You can still have fun and always be aware of potential event issues at the same time. After a few events on high alert, you will casually remain cognizant of the surroundings without compromising your enjoyment. When you are on self-high alertness, you may notice someone fully clothed in the summer with a heavy backpack. You may notice a person packing a firearm; you may witness that person actually pulling out that firearm before anyone else notices.

Although 99.99% of the time nothing as significant as a mass shooting may happen from what you notice, your self-high alert mode gives you a head start and survival advantage if something ever does occur. An unexpected mass shooting can compare to an unexpected natural disaster; there are no guarantees of outcome but the decision-making structures are important for survival of a disaster (Gainsborough, n.d.). You are your decision making structure. Being on high alert at events is a part of your structure.

Pay attention. If you go with friends have a designated person that pays attention comparable to having a designated driver. Imagine being able to have a friend that notifies you right away after noticing someone walking in a club with a firearm pulled out. You find out immediately versus dancing, drinking, and partying extra minutes/seconds, which may be crucial for your survival.

A designated "alert" person may appear too much effort but if you are ever in a situation such as a mass shooting, you will appreciate such effort. Alert mode helps survive other attacks too such as knife attacks, bomb attacks, and other weaponry attacks. You owe it to your life to stay on alert; do not simply rely on event security.

Step

#3

How to Survive a Mass Shooting

NO HESITATION

What I learned from being an unwilling participant in mass shootings is that you must take decisive action immediately. Do not hesitate with whatever choice you make for the moment. That time when my friend shoved me to the ground, he did it quickly and immediately without hesitation. It may have saved my life too.

I did not mention it earlier but two people experienced bullet wounds at that game and only one survived. Going to the ground as quickly as my friend and I did may have saved us. There were no explanations and no curiosity questions. After the first gunshot, there was quick action.

Fast action is what I took from that point forward. If ever at an event where a crowd shooting occurred, as stated there were many shooting events within my inner city environment, I responded quickly without trying to make reasoning and understanding of the moment. You can discover the issue, find out who, what, why, and how later. There have been a

How to Survive a Mass Shooting

few times that I have gone to the ground after hearing fireworks and others laughed at me, but I would rather get those laughs than be standing when split second bullets are coming.

Be a leader in a mass shooting situation and do not make indecisive decisions because the boldest decisions are the safest (Arsham, n.d.).

Step

#4

GROUND CONTROL

Already mentioned, if ever you hear what you think are gunshots at an event you attend get on the ground ASAP! Do not start running. Simply get on the ground. Yes, I have experienced ridicule for doing this too quickly when those gunshots turned out to be fireworks or toy poppers. However, I have witnessed praised also for getting to the ground swiftly because it signaled to others to get down as well during real live shootings.

When you get down try not to panic. Quickly recognize and count the number of gunshots. Counting the number of gunshots helps keep your mental awareness and helps keep you in control of an uncontrollable situation. There are times when a shooter is driving by and there are times when a shooter is walking up. When you get to the ground try and understand what type of shooting you have. A drive by or a walk up (also stationary).

From experiences, if it is a drive-by just stay on the ground and you should be safe

How to Survive a Mass Shooting

after a few minutes max time. Do not stay standing or start running during a drive-by. Belief it or not drive-by mass shootings offers you a greater chance of survival. Stay on the ground and wait.

Obviously, walk up shootings or stationary shootings put you at greater risk of non-survival. This is why you need to keep your head raised slightly when you initially get on the ground, count gunshots, and run away (Responding, n.d.) as soon as you hear a break in gunshots. If all else fails play dead. There are instances where people have survived mass shootings by playing dead. Personally, I will make playing dead my very last resort of survival.

Step #5

How to Survive a Mass Shooting

RUN

Here is a powerful three-letter word as it relates to a mass shooting, RUN. When it is time to run, run. Once you quickly identify there is no drive by shooting and that someone is shooting consistently from afar or walking up, then get off the ground and start running!

Where do you run? How far do you run? What do you do after you are in a safe place? Should you help others? All of these questions should have personal answers identified by you when you get an understanding of the event as stated in Step 1.

When you get an understanding of your activity, you will know when, and where to run and any other particulars you establish. Whatever you determine, running is an essential step with survival of any active ongoing mass shooting (Active Shooter, n.d.). When you decide to run, do it without hesitation as described in Step 3.

Step #6

HIDE

If for some reason the situation does not allow you to run, you need to hide! You should already know the best places to hide from getting an understanding. Take decisive action and hide since you are unable to run.

In many instances, hiding is just enough to deter an active shooter because time is of the essence. Law enforcement responses to shootings are becoming faster and faster. Shooters are aware of this so hiding for even a short period may help you survive a scary mass shooting.

When you hide, turn out the lights, barricade doors, stay low, and find any objects that will help you defend yourself (Active Shooter, n.d.). One of the first things taught to me when I began teaching was to look and find places you and your students can hide in case of an active shooter situation. Hiding is a valued way of surviving and is a recommendation by many people in law enforcement.

Always remember, if your situation prevents you from taking off like a cheetah then you need to hide like an artic fox.

Step #7

How to Survive a Mass Shooting

LOCK AND BARRICADE

Locking doors and creating barricades will help you survive. The more obstacles and hurdles a shooter has to overcome will benefit your life. It does not take long to discover what may be necessary if a shooting situation occurs.

Furniture, appliances, and equipment is useful when creating a barricade. Many doors have locks so do not overlook the fact of locking a door. After you lock and barricade, look for a way to escape. If there are no ways to escape, prepare yourself mentally and get ready to fight!

Step
#8

How to Survive a Mass Shooting

ATTACK

After you have hidden, locked the doors and barricaded, prepare yourself for the fight of your life. Literally, locate any object you can use and get ready for an attack. If there is more than one person with you, you increase your chances of survival by attacking.

Do not sit back and wait once the obvious fight is right before you. Be proactive and go down fighting. The idea that a shooter will pass you by may be a futile idea. Do not leave your survival in the hands of a shooter. Take charge with decisive decision-making and throw/use everything possible at the shooter. Do escape if there is any window of opportunity for escape during the fight but make no mistake about it, attack when it is time to attack. Your attack of the shooter may save the lives of others as well.

Step #9

How to Survive a Mass Shooting

CONCEAL CARRY

This step does not advocate for or against gun control. Simply stated there may be no better way to survive a mass shooting than to return fire. The ability to return fire changes the entire dynamics of a mass shooting experience. There have been instances of inner city shootings where almost immediately return fire happened.

Owning a concealed firearm will help you survive but it comes with certain responsibilities. If you choose to own a firearm to protect yourself at events, be sure to get all the legal details and requirements from your local state government. Many events do not allow firearms and there are serious consequences for carrying a firearm illegally so make sure you get a full understanding BEFOREHAND if you choose to exercise this right to help you survive a mass shooting. Take required classes and learn how to shoot accurately. Educate yourself thoroughly on the responsible use of a firearm.

This book is about what you can do to survive a mass shooting and not about whether a gunman or you should have access to guns. The issue of gun control is one of the most debated issues in my lifetime. Many myths surround the issue of gun control (TEN MYTHS, n.d.) so trying to make a case for or against it within this little work is asinine.

Nonetheless, it is foolhardy not to mention the aspect of being able to return accurate fire as a real way to survive if you are ever in a shooting quagmire. Common sense tells you that it is better to have the ability to return fire than not have that ability especially if you are ever in an active shooter situation.

Step #10

How to Survive a Mass Shooting

STAY CALM

Staying calm during a crisis such as a mass shooting will help you make better decisions (Masullo, 2014). The immediate decisions you make are detrimental to your survival and possibly the survival of others. Quickly recognize what is happening, take quick action, and stay calm.

In a bad scenario where you are shot, remain calm and focus on what you can do to survive. The words "stay calm" are easier to write and say than to physically do. This is why you should play out scenarios in your head BEFORE you go to any event.

Not panicking assists with your breathing efforts and thinking about what you can do to survive will keep you alive.

OUTRO

By reading this little work, you have taken the first step of surviving a mass shooting. Now you can safely attend events without compromising your ability to have a good time.

You will survive a mass shooting if you get an understanding of the event, be on high alert, have no hesitation, hit the ground when necessary, run, hide, attack, return fire, and stay calm!

References:

Active Shooter. (n.d.). Retrieved July 30, 2016, from https://protect.iu.edu/emergency-planning/procedures/active-shooter.html

Arsham, H., Professor. (n.d.). Leadership Decision Making. Retrieved July 30, 2016, from http://home.ubalt.edu/ntsbarsh/opre640/partXIII.htm

Dealing with Culture Shock. (n.d.). Retrieved July 26, 2016, from http://web.iit.edu/study-abroad/students-abroad/dealing-culture-shock

Gainsborough, J. (n.d.). Surviving Natural Disaster. Retrieved July 30, 2016, from http://www.bentley.edu/impact/articles/surviving-natural-disaster

Masullo, K. (2014, January 25). Leadership during Crisis. Retrieved July

30, 2016, from
http://sites.psu.edu/leadership/2014/01/
25/leadership-during-crisis/

Responding To An Active Shooter On
Campus. (n.d.). Retrieved July 30, 2016,
from
https://www.ohio.edu/police/tips/actives
hooter.cfm

TEN MYTHS ABOUT GUN CONTROL.
(n.d.). Retrieved July 30, 2016, from
http://people.duke.edu/~gnsmith/article
s/myths.htm

About The Author

Walter Hebrew is one of the pen names for Walter Anderson. He is the son of a disabled war veteran, an educator, author, father, and diverse entrepreneur. Formally educated in Chemistry (B.S.), and Higher Education (M.S.), he shares his time between helping college students, high school students, and creating interesting projects. His intellectual portfolio includes books (exclusive, limited prints), entertainment, and more.

Published by Hood Theorem

Contact the author via the email or contact form at HoodTheorem.com

WITHDRAWN

CPSIA information can be obtained
at www.ICGtesting.com
Printed in the USA
LVHW081153150819
627630LV00011BA/459/P